IMAGES
of America

CORTLANDT

IMAGES
of America

CORTLANDT

Laura Lee M. Keating and
Jean M. Moczarski

ARCADIA
PUBLISHING

Published by Arcadia Publishing
Charleston, South Carolina

Library of Congress Control Number: 2013930893

For all general information, please contact Arcadia Publishing:
Telephone 843-853-2070
Fax 843-853-0044
E-mail sales@arcadiapublishing.com
For customer service and orders:
Toll-Free 1-888-313-2665

Visit us on the Internet at www.arcadiapublishing.com

Dedicated to Craig L. Keating and Peter J. Moczarski, Jr.—
husbands in name and love—patient supporters at heart.

CONTENTS

ACKNOWLEDGMENTS

This visual, historic tour of the town of Cortlandt and its environs would not have been possible without the guidance, support and wonderful visits with many people. We have done our best to accurately identify the people and places presented.

The Hendrick Hudson Free Library's director, Jill Davis, assured us that this title would be a welcome addition to the library's collection and is eagerly awaiting its release.

The staff at Peekskill's Field Library, including director Sibyl Canaan, head of reference Robert Boyle, reference librarian and local history specialist Kim Stucko, and Harni Evans shared their treasured collections while offering words of wisdom and encouragement.

Betty Travis at Buchanan Village Hall opened the William J. Burke History Collection to us, trusting us with many photographs, whether they were in frames or files.

Residents Barbara Annichairico, Diane Edwards Tangen, Judy O'Brien, Tommy and Trish Cole, Richard Fay, Henry "Hank" Reynolds, Tina Rickett, Jeff Canning, and Cheryl and William "Bill" Murray shared their local stories, as well as interest in this project.

Peekskill city historian John Curran opened the Peekskill Museum's massive archives to us with enthusiasm and great support. Lorman "Augie" Augustowski lent us his calm professionalism.

John Marvin of Pronto Printer guided us in the early days of the scanning process.

Thanks also to William Florence for his legal guidance and wisdom as well as local history stories.

INTRODUCTION

The town of Cortlandt is not a single entity but is made up of several hamlets and two villages and is quite diverse both economically and socially. It is located in the northwest corner of Westchester County, New York. New York State was one of the 13 original colonies. New York became an independent state on July 9, 1776, and enacted its constitution in 1777. Gov. George Clinton, one of the first governors of New York, declared Cortlandt a town in 1788, when the county was divided into 20 townships. The content of this book will attempt to discuss the historical and cultural aspects of the town of Cortlandt. We will explore the place names of the various parts of the town, their origins, special and unique people, and significant historical events that shaped the town.

The town of Cortlandt comprises an area of 34.5 square miles and has a population of approximately 38,000 people. The landforms are mostly hilly, rocky outcrops with many ponds and lakes. The town of Cortlandt works diligently to preserve green space and natural areas while, at the same time, encouraging industrial and community development. The specific parts of the town of Cortlandt this book focuses on are Montrose, Buchanan, Verplanck, Croton-on-Hudson, Crugers, Cortlandt Manor, and VanCortlandtville. Many of these villages and hamlets contain century-old beautiful architecture and have been historically preserved by local governments. These structures represent a bygone era yet complement modern living.

Whether you were born and raised in the town of Cortlandt or have joined these communities later, you will enjoy visiting historic and unique places and people. Having recently celebrated the Hudson-Fulton-Champlain Quadricentennial in 2009, Cortlandt is keenly aware of its place in the Hudson River valley's past, present, and future. It is inherently important for the people of a community to learn about the area in which they live and understand how its history has created current cultures and traditions. Cortlandt is a complex town with a variety of communities that provide an interesting mix of cultures and people. With its variety of communities, it is easy for folks to find a home that suits their lifestyles. Within Images of America: Cortlandt, you will find countless photographs of the many different people and places that make up the town. You, as the reader, will also make discoveries of the many little-known facts and events that have shaped the town of Cortlandt.

The town borders the Hudson River in Verplanck, which lends itself to many, many nautical stories and pictures. The village of Buchanan also has a long history in relation to the former Indian Point amusement areas, which is now home to the Entergy Nuclear Power Plant. The hamlet of Montrose was named for the Montross family. Through the incorporated villages of Croton-on-Hudson and Buchanan and the hamlet of Montrose are the major roadways of Routes 9 and 9A. Route 9 is named the Albany Post Road and was the original route from New York City to Albany. At various times in American history, it also served as an early postal and carriage route.

Another major roadway, Route 6 traverses the town from west to east. From the Hudson River to the city of Peekskill, East Route 6 is home to countless businesses in the town of Cortlandt and is referred to as "Cortlandt Boulevard." The present Cortlandt Town Center houses a variety of stores serving many needs such as food, clothing, literature, and home decor. This vibrant shopping center includes a movie theater complex.

Also along Route 6 is Michael Mongero Memorial Park with its monuments listing local military veterans; the park is the site of annual commemorations honoring those veterans both living and dead. Located off Route 6 on Westbrook Drive is the Muriel Morabito Community Center, which welcomes seniors for weekly meals and activities. It is also used as an emergency disaster center. Former town clerk Muriel Morabito is pictured among our images. There are also 24 parks and recreation venues, of various sizes, within the town.

It also should be noted that the Peekskill-Cortlandt area, besides having historical significance, is poised to be reinvigorated as a thriving tourist spot. All the hamlets and villages in the town of Cortlandt realize what a treasure the Hudson River is, as well as our proximity to New York City.

There is a wealth of history within the town of Cortlandt, and parts of its history date back to when the Dutch settled the town.

Cortlandt derives its name from the Dutch VanCortlandt family, who began purchasing land in 1677 from the Croton River north to Anthony's Nose and east to what is now Connecticut. The Dutch presence in New York is reflected in its former name New Amsterdam. After the British took control of New Amsterdam from the Dutch, the colony was renamed New York. Both English and Dutch influences remain strong. Many towns, families, streets, and so on carry Dutch and British place names to this day.

In early Dutch history, another wealthy landowner was Frederick Philipse, and his Philipsburg Manor bordered the VanCortlandt Manor where the Croton River meets the Hudson River. Both of these affluent and influential Dutch landowners had profitable businesses in the early to mid-1600s and 1700s. The area the town of Cortlandt encompasses is a descendant of these early manors.

Cortlandt was significant during battles of the American Revolution. Cortlandt's participation in the American Revolution was the beginning of many times when its citizenry would serve America.

Education has always been a part of the formation of the town of Cortlandt. Within the town are two school districts, Lakeland Central School District and Hendrick Hudson School District. Lakeland includes the following schools: George Washington Elementary, Lincoln-Titus Elementary, VanCortlandtville Elementary, Walter Panas High School, and Lakeland High School. Within the Hendrick Hudson district are the following schools: Furnace Woods Elementary, Buchanan-Verplanck Elementary, Frank G. Lindsey Elementary, Blue Mountain Middle, and Hendrick Hudson High School.

Another interesting fact about education concerns the village of Buchanan. The village was one of the first municipalities in New York State to establish a school in 1831. This was done after the New York State Legislature enacted a law creating a public education system in the state. This legislation was passed in 1812. All the school districts in the town of Cortlandt are required to teach and emphasize local New York history as part of their elementary curriculum, and this volume could be a valuable asset to our schools.

One

THE TOWN OF CORTLANDT
AND VANCORTLANDTVILLE

Cortlandt is bounded on the west by the Hudson River, the north by Putnam County, and the east by the two incorporated villages of Buchanan and Croton-on-Hudson and the hamlets of Montrose, Crugers, and Verplanck. After the town was created and Phillip VanCortlandt became the first town supervisor, growth was steady, which continues to this day.

The early 19th century brought industrialization to the area of the town of Cortlandt known as Verplanck. The hamlet began to prosper as a brick-making center. The town of Cortlandt, in the late 19th and early 20th centuries, had many seasonal bungalows catering to the wealthy who traveled north on the early Hudson River railroads. After World War II, as in many other parts of New York State, suburbanization of the town rapidly led to many residents commuting to the major employment centers of White Plains, the county seat, and New York City.

The area of the town of Cortlandt known as VanCortlandtville was a strategic focal point in the American Revolution with great historical significance. The entire area is sometimes referred to as the gateway to the "Hudson Highlands."

Of note within VanCortlandtville are St. Peter's Church and Cemetery, the VanCortlandt Upper Manor House, the Little Red Schoolhouse, and Cortlandt Town Hall, which was originally the VanCortlandtville School.

St. Peter's Church was dedicated in 1767 and served as a field hospital during the American Revolution. Among those buried in the adjoining cemetery are Revolutionary War soldiers, including John Paulding, who was one of the captors of Maj. John André, a British spy. Also buried there are two members of the 54th Massachusetts US Colored Troops who fought gallantly during the Civil War.

The VanCortlandt Upper Manor House was used many times by George Washington and his officers from 1776 through 1778. It is now a health care facility.

The Little Red Schoolhouse is believed to be the site of an early Baptist church. This one-room schoolhouse was built in the early 1800s and is next to St. Peter's Church and Cemetery. The school was closed in 1935, reopened in 1952, and operated until 1970. It is now a museum maintained by the VanCortlandtville Historical Society.

The Bear Mountain Bridge and Road were built between 1923 and 1924. The project, which cost more than $4 million, was funded by a group of investors headed by Averell Harriman's brother Edward Roland Harriman. Folklore tells that the bridge and road were designed to make it more convenient for family and friends on the other side of the Hudson River to visit Edward's wife, Gladys. Today, its toll is little more than $1 only in one direction, making it one of New York transportation's great values. This c. 1940 photograph shows a group of bridge workers assembled on the "Goat Trail," now known as the Camp Smith Trail. It is so called because it borders on the Camp Smith military base. The New York–New Jersey Trail Conference maintains this intermediate hiking trail. (Courtesy of Barbara Annichairico.)

This postcard, published by the Valentine & Sons Publishing Company in New York and Boston, shows the early, humble days of life on the shores of Annsville Creek. (Courtesy of Laura Lee M. Keating.)

Many residents of the Hudson River municipalities within the town of Cortlandt fashioned houseboats along the shoreline. The structure at the center of this image could be one of them. (Courtesy of the Field Library Historical Collection, The Colin T. Naylor Jr. Archives and the Peekskill Museum.)

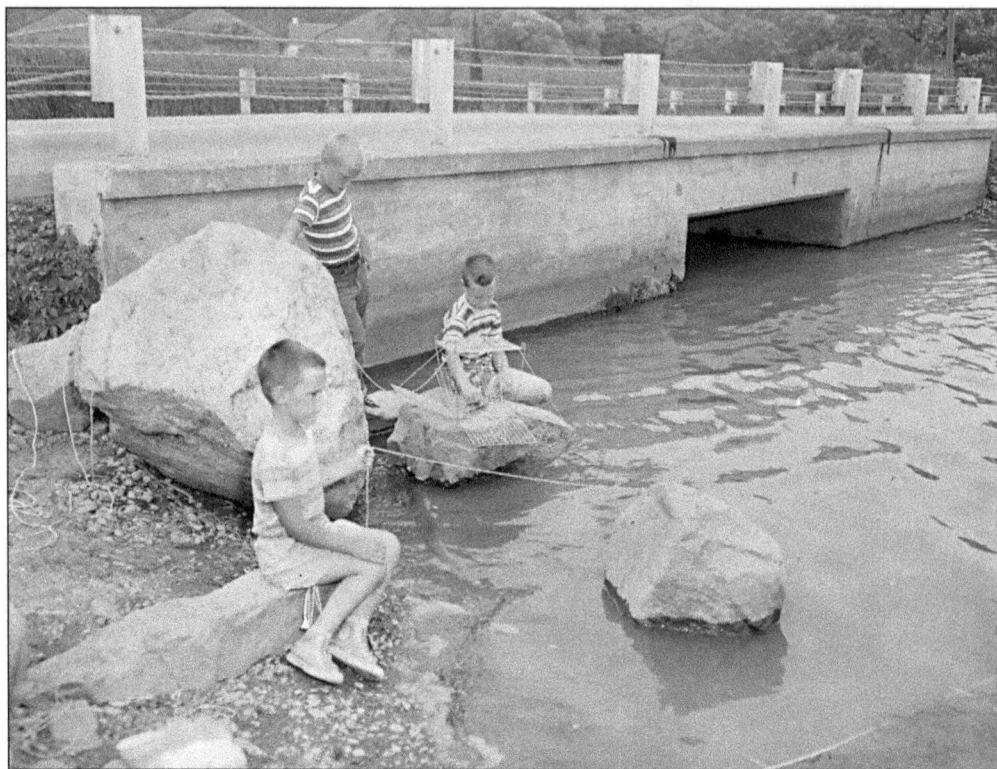

From left to right, eight-year-old Richard Bobay, James Bobay, and six-year-old Kevin Scaury enjoy a relaxing day of crabbing at Roa Hook in July 1958. This area borders Annsville Creek near Camp Smith. The origin of the name Roa Hook is unknown; however, Annsville Creek is named for Anne VanCortlandt, an early member of Cortlandt's founding family. Today, one can cross the Annsville Creek over the small Annsville Bridge and still see people crabbing. (Courtesy of the Peekskill Museum.)

Ray Kuty is enthused by his success at crabbing at Annsville Creek in August 1954. Harvesting these popular crustaceans fed locals in the past and continues to do so today. (Courtesy of the Peekskill Museum.)

Shown at peace in March 1937 is Gallows Hill Bridge. During the American Revolution, and in sharp contrast to what is pictured, this bridge played the role of executioner of those betraying the patriot cause. (Courtesy of the Cortlandt Museum.)

Watch Hill was the home of Angus Sutherland, a Tory whose brother Alexander commanded the ship *Vulture*, which carried Maj. John André. The major would later partner with Benedict Arnold in a famous betrayal during the American Revolution. (Courtesy of the Cortlandt Museum.)

Grand Old Party (GOP) town clerk Muriel Morabito is flanked by GOP assemblyman Peter Biondo, left, and state senator Bernard G. Gordon at the annual Cortlandt GOP dinner in October 1967. (Courtesy of the Peekskill Museum.)

This is Cub Scout Pack No. 145 based in VanCortlandville at its Scouts award dinner on February 17, 1950. (Courtesy of Jeff Canning and the VanCortlandville Historical Society.)

This is the first combined graduating class in the new VanCortlandtville School, on June 18, 1937, after consolidation with Annsville, including the Continental Village. The children are (first row) Gloria Morley, Gladys Gaudineer, Christine Conway, Herbert O'Dell, Douglas Mowbray, and Harold Smith; (second row) Sylvia Fowler, Marjorie Conley, Doris Emaus, Gene Smith, and Edward Avery; (third row) Marion Beisser, Evelyn Puff, Evelyn Booth, Stephen Tintor, Albert Beisser, and John Thomas. (Courtesy of Jeff Canning and the VanCortlandtville Historical Society.)

Two

THE VILLAGES OF BUCHANAN AND CROTON-ON-HUDSON

The village of Buchanan is located northeast of Verplanck on the eastern bank of the Hudson River. Located south of the city of Peekskill, it comprises 1.5 square miles; has approximately 2,200 residents, numerous businesses, and public services; and is within the Hendrick Hudson School District.

Buchanan's original name was East Haverstraw. When a railroad station was built at the end of White Street in 1848, the stop was called East Haverstaw. Later, the station was moved to Montrose, and the village became known as Centerville because it was halfway between Verplanck and Peekskill. It was eventually named Buchanan after the first postmaster, George Buchanan. Its first mayor, Augustus Cole, was a community and business leader.

Buchanan was also one of the first communities in New York State to provide a school building after the state legislature had established a statewide school system in 1812. The first school was built in 1831.

In 1924, Indian Point Park was acquired by the Hudson River Day Line, which supported both boat travel and a thriving amusement park until 1954. It is now the site of a nuclear power plant operated by Entergy.

The village of Croton-on-Hudson was incorporated in 1898. Residents farmed, worked in the brickyards at Croton Point, or on the railroad. With the construction of the Croton Dam in the early 1900s, the village grew in population. The Croton Dam was one of the largest masonry dams ever built, and the water supply serves nearby New York City and Westchester County.

Croton-on-Hudson is a small village despite its proximity to New York City. It is a river town that retains its early charm with many small shops, restaurants, and businesses. There are several boatyards, marinas, and a sailing school. Residents enjoy waterfront parkland and river access. Croton still has spectacular vistas, as it did in 1609, when Henry Hudson discovered the Hudson River.

The Croton-Harmon railroad station serves as a hub for both Metro-North and Amtrak rail services. Businessman and land developer Clifford B. Harmon is the station's namesake.

Here is the Buchanan School in 1908. The Buchanan Village Hall now occupies this site. Located at Tate Avenue and near Buchanan Circle, it was the original site of the halfway house between New York City and Kingston, New York, which was the first capital of New York State. (Donated by Vera and Fred Haege to the William J. Burke Collection at Buchanan Village Hall.)

Two soldiers in uniform, from left to right, Hayden and Glynn Price, stand at attention before serving their country overseas during World War I. (Courtesy of Cheryl and William Murray.)

Glynn Price is pictured here in uniform and is set to blow his bugle. This photograph was taken at camp in Spartanburg, South Carolina, during World War I. Price was a native of Buchanan, New York. (Courtesy of Cheryl and William Murray.)

Pictured here is Hayden Price in full military uniform. This picture was taken in France in 1918. (Courtesy of Cheryl and William Murray.)

The staff of the Standard Coated Products plant takes time from the workday to pose for this photograph in 1924. Note the vested suits and hats, which were the style of the time. (Donated by Charles Welsch to the William J. Burke History Room at Buchanan Village Hall.)

Employees of Standard Coated Products company are, from left to right, (first row) unidentified, George Buchanan Sr., Harold S. Hull, Henry M. Garlick, Alvin Hunsicker, W.E. Thatcher, and D. Allen; (second row) W.B. Fenton, J.T. Broadbent, Henry Pope, P.A. Bivens, B.H. Atha, Charles Del Orme, Charles Nourse, J. Wilson, W. Klee, R. Ferrar, I. Kip, George Buchanan Jr., D. Allen Jr., T. Coulter, H. Suidall, unidentified, H. Hyatt, and T. VanOrden; (third row) G. Newton, H. Jung, M. King, unidentified, B. Daly, unidentified, J. Newman Sr., E. Frohner, F. Lent, and F. Gilman. Those in the top left corner are J. Hardee, C. Quick. (Courtesy of the William J. Burke History Room at Buchanan Village Hall.)

The Standard Coated Products construction workers pose for this photograph in 1910. Wearing hats, these sturdy men are as proud to be a part of this revolutionary enterprise as the suited men in previous images. Note the small "x" on the image of the gentleman in the center of this photograph. Could this be a relative of the photograph's donor, Mrs. Elbert Smith? (Donated by Mrs. Elbert Smith to the William J. Burke History Room at Buchanan Village Hall.)

Picnics were among many recreational activities that marked Buchanan's social life in the early 1900s. An area known as Midway Oval hosted many local baseball games. Electric Park was home to an amusement park, theater, and dance pavilion. (Courtesy of Cheryl and William Murray.)

This image shows deputy sheriffs in Buchanan in the 1890s. The Buchanan Police Department was formed in 1928. They would meet their first police chief in 1929. (Courtesy of Cheryl and William Murray.)

According to "Bud" Edwards's daughter Diane, her father was a dedicated and reliable local businessman. His station, located near Buchanan Circle, w–as a place where the community could be assured of honest, good service on their automobiles. (Both, courtesy of Diane Edwards Tangen.)

During wartime, families supported each other in order to keep homes and communities thriving. In peacetime, those strong relationships continued. (Courtesy of Diane Edwards Tangen.)

The Edwards Gas Station was located at the corner of Albany Post Road and Tate Avenue in Buchanan. Elmer Edwards's daughter Diane Edwards Tangen remembers her dad's business warmly. (Courtesy of Diane Edwards Tangen.)

This 1920s image shows workers in front of the Buchanan Garage. From left to right are Buddy ?, Henry ?, Howard Conklin, Gus Cole, and Jacob Cole. The original stone building still exists and is located at Buchanan Circle. (Courtesy of Cheryl and William Murray.)

The village of Buchanan in 1928 was the home of Ida and Arthur Conklin's hardware store. Small by today's standards yet packed with whatever was needed to build and maintain a home, business, house of worship, or school, this was one of a number of commercial enterprises now fondly called mom-and-pop stores, which were cornerstones in America. They are the ancestors of today's big box stores and national chains. They held onto their uniqueness because they were operated and patronized by local citizens. The year 1928 proved to be a busy year for Arthur Conklin. He was elected a village trustee, along with Leonard Tuttle, Charles Brenning, and Joseph Yafcak. Buchanan is still home to many businesses, such as the Buchanan Home Center and the Entergy Nuclear Power Plant. (Courtesy of the William J. Burke Collection at Buchanan Village Hall.)

Pictured are the sons of Augustus "Gus" Cole, the first mayor of Buchanan. They are, from left to right, Vernon, Sheldon, and Clayton Cole. (Courtesy of Tina Rickett.)

Blue- and white-collar workers came together in this photograph, showing how partnership and teamwork brought success to the American Oil Company. (Courtesy of Tina Rickett.)

Augustus Cole is shown here proudly serving his country as a member of the US Navy. (Courtesy of Tina Rickett.)

A Texaco gas pump, located in Buchanan, is evidence of the early expansion of the automobile industry in New York and the country. Buchanan Circle is located in the village and the local post office still stands in this area. (Courtesy of Tina Rickett and Cheryl and William Murray.)

The automobile grew from its earliest days as the horseless carriage to a viable industry throughout America and the world. Auto dealership employees enjoy a night away from the pressures of the business. Augustus Cole is second from the right in this image. (Courtesy of Tina Rickett.)

Pictured here is a local business leader of Buchanan, Gus Cole. His automobile business expanded under his leadership. The dealership included the car model, Packard, which was built in Detroit, Michigan. Cole would often drive the car back from the Midwest to his dealership. He was a president of the Lincoln Society in Peekskill, which is the oldest Lincoln Society in America, founded in 1903. (Courtesy of Tina Rickett.)

This smiling, well-dressed couple enjoys life in Buchanan in the last century. (Courtesy of Cheryl and William Murray.)

Trinity Boscobel Church in Buchanan still stands and is an active church today. This church was established in 1854. (Courtesy of Cheryl and William Murray.)

The Buchanan Athletic Club's baseball team in May 1938 showed that this community could play as hard as it worked. Some team members are Joseph Brigsey Nohai, Peter Obuhanich, Bertram Tomlinson, Ray Travis, John Morgan, John Polinsky, Francis Lent, and Edward Callahan. (Courtesy of the Cortlandt Museum.)

These Buchanan Boy Scouts in April 1938 learn and share community pride. Members are, from left to right, (first row) Fred Mitchell, Jack Mitchell, Bob Segnit, Jim Macauley, Joe DiPietro, and Don Lane; (second row) George Calley, John Mallas, and Frank Sutterby. (Courtesy of the Cortlandt Museum.)

The 1943–1944 first-grade class of Buchanan Grammar School sits very properly for this picture. Students are, from left to right, (first row) Peggy Werder, Beryl Chase, Patricia Clamberlain, Carol Raymond, Marie Ansted, Diane Edwards, Lois Linder, and Maryann Cooney; (second row) Michael Rodak, Billy ?, Joe Leverich, and Joe Rohrick; (third row) Gilbert Bauer, Joseph Butler, Walter Van Tassel, Bobby Conklin, and Ralph Ferrussi. (Courtesy of Diane Edwards Tangen.)

Pictured here is Buchanan Engine's first marching band. It was formed on September 11, 1943. Members are shown practicing at their Bleakley Avenue firehouse. (Courtesy of Cheryl and William Murray.)

A clambake is held at Lounsbury Pond in Blue Mountain Park in September 1919. The Sick Benefit Society donor was Howard Conklin. Those who attended this clambake were employees of Standard Coated Products. On the left are Bill Tompkins (who hosted the bake), Frank Bennett, Howard Conklin, Bert Travis, Frank Wilke, Tom Coulter, Fred Ingold, and George Welch. In the front is Henry Junoe. On the right are Len Tuttle, Charlie Lent (a sheriff), John Tuttle, Ed Hoeffley, William Noe, Oss Lent, Charlie Gilman, Barney Daley, Ed Lent, Mack McCormick, Judge King, Len Conklin, and Ardron Horton. In the front is John Clune. (Courtesy of the William J. Burke History Collection at Buchanan Village Hall.)

Pictured here is a local woman enjoying the fresh air and nature so typical of Cortlandt in the early 20th century. (Courtesy of Judy O'Brien.)

This Buy Rite Discount Kiddieland was part of a popular amusement park along the Hudson River. It included a nursery, children's rides, and discount produce. (Courtesy of Henry Reynolds.)

Buchanan mothers had many choices for their children's recreation because of the many facilities that began developing in the early 1900s. Among them were a baseball field, a basketball court, a children's playground, and, finally in 1965, two tennis courts. (Courtesy of Cheryl and William Murray.)

The steamboat *Mary Powell*, which plied the Hudson River between Kingston, New York, and New York City, often stopped at Verplanck and Buchanan. (Courtesy of Henry Reynolds.)

The Iron Steamboat Company provided ferry service on the Hudson River. (Courtesy of Henry Reynolds.)

The steamer *Watch Hill* is shown here docked near Oscawana Island in Crugers. It was owned and operated by the Ripley family. (Courtesy of Henry Reynolds.)

The Day Liner *Albany* makes its way past Indian Point in 1928. (Donated by Alice and Robert Reese to the William J. Burke History Collection at Buchanan Village Hall.)

This postcard of the Old Post Inn in Croton shows lodging that dated back to the 18th century. This inn was on Grand Street and fell victim to fire some years ago. (Courtesy of the Cortlandt Museum.)

This image of Chimney Corner Cabin at the junction of Albany Post Road and Furnace Dock Road in Croton in 1950 shows a quaint establishment, which has undergone numerous changes and is currently a Mexican restaurant. (Courtesy of the Cortlandt Museum.)

The Watergate Motor Hotel in Croton boasted 43 ultra-modern rooms, free television, air-conditioning, tile showers, boating, bathing, and fishing on a private lake while maintaining its aura of country-club living. It also noted its one-hour proximity to New York City's exciting Times Square. (Courtesy of the Cortlandt Museum.)

Ruins of Bailey Wire Works are seen here after the first Croton Dam broke in 1841. The Bailey Wire Works was part of the Baily Wire Mill. (Courtesy of the Cortlandt Museum.)

The Wire Mill Bridge is shown here before 1841; it crossed the Croton River near present-day Route 9. (Courtesy of the Cortlandt Museum.)

In 1910, in the Harmon section of Croton-on-Hudson, a racetrack was a popular local venue. The track was located near present day Route 9, which runs from New York City to Albany, the state's capital. (Courtesy of the Cortlandt Museum.)

Three

THE HAMLET OF CRUGERS

Crugers, an area within the town of Cortlandt, lies below the hamlet of Montrose and hugs the Hudson River just north of Croton-on-Hudson. The area lies just off Albany Post Road, a major thoroughfare in the town and in Westchester County. Crugers developed as a mainly residential area with small housing developments interspersed with large, former estates.

The Cruger family dates to the early 16th century and was involved with early colonial politics. In fact, John Cruger II served as the mayor of New York from 1756 through 1765. At the turn of the 19th century, a prominent family, the Ripley family acquired a large amount of property. Also at that time, Oscawana Island, an area once inhabited by Native Americans, became a popular spot for boaters on the Hudson River. There also was a ferry that ran between Haverstraw, across the river, to Cruger's (as it was then spelled). Joseph Ripley, an artesian well businessman, operated a little ferry boat known as the *Watch Hill*.

After World War II, the area known as Crugers experienced development and growth. By 1940, the US government wanted the property, which was over 200 acres and owned by the Dyckman family, to build a veterans' hospital and facility. On the property was a huge mansion, known as the Boscobel mansion, which was dismantled and moved to Garrison, New York, where it stands today.

Presently, the homes and neighborhoods of the area known as Crugers serve a population largely made up of commuters traveling to New York City or down county to White Plains. Crugers is located within the Hendrick Hudson School District. The small area has local businesses, stores, and access to the major south highway of Route 9.

New York Central Railroad workers pose in front of a tunnel they are digging near Oscawana Island in Crugers. The tunnel would expand railroad travel to Peekskill and northern Westchester County and increase prosperity in the town of Cortlandt. Today, the Metro-North Railroad carries approximately 30,000 passengers daily to Grand Central Terminal in New York City, which celebrates its 100th anniversary in 2013. (Courtesy of Henry Reynolds.)

Early indoor plumbing meant families had to drill artesian wells to get their water. The Ripley family developed this thriving business in Crugers and Ossining, New York. (Courtesy of Henry Reynolds.)

Pictured are two original photographs
of Edwin Ripley's artesian well business.
The property of the Ripley family
in Crugers was quite extensive. The
property had large homes and was located
on the shores of the Hudson River.
Ripley made his fortune in drilling wells
for the early homeowners of this area.
(Both, courtesy of Henry Reynolds.)

Here is one of the many large homes surrounding the Ripley family property. The gabled roofs and front porches display architectural features of a bygone era. (Courtesy of Henry Reynolds.)

The architectural styles pictured here include gabled roofs and ornate decorations. The styles were brought over from Europe and incorporated into American building designs. At that time, homes were quite spacious, housing large families as well as extended families. (Courtesy of Henry Reynolds.)

Women of the Ripley family show their progressive side in their leisure interests by using binoculars and apparently smoking a pipe! (Courtesy of Henry Reynolds.)

This is a June 10, 1900, scene from Crugers Hill, now the present Veterans Administration property, which is also known as Franklin Delano Roosevelt Healthcare. Edwin Ripley took the photograph. (Courtesy of Henry Reynolds.)

The photograph shows open land in Crugers. It was later to become one of the many suburban areas of the town used for extensive commuting to New York City. (Courtesy of Henry Reynolds.)

Twilight falls on early riverside industry in the town of Cortlandt. Industrialization grew along waterways, especially the Hudson River, because of access to the Erie Canal and points west and because this type of transportation was cheap. (Courtesy of Henry Reynolds.)

This is the Crugers railroad station on the New York Central Railroad line. (Courtesy of Henry Reynolds.)

Pictured here is possibly Edwin Ripley on the porch of his home in Crugers. This photograph may have been taken in the early 20th century. (Courtesy of Henry Reynolds.)

Mabel B. Palmer Ripley, once one of the oldest residents of the town of Cortlandt, died at her home in Crugers on August 11, 1965, at the age of 91. She was the wife of prominent businessman Edwin Ripley, who drilled many artesian wells in Cortlandt and in Putnam County. (Courtesy of Henry Reynolds.)

Croton River Bridge
1894

Pictured is the original wooden Croton River Bridge in 1894. Croton River is a tributary of the Hudson River. (Courtesy of Henry Reynolds.)

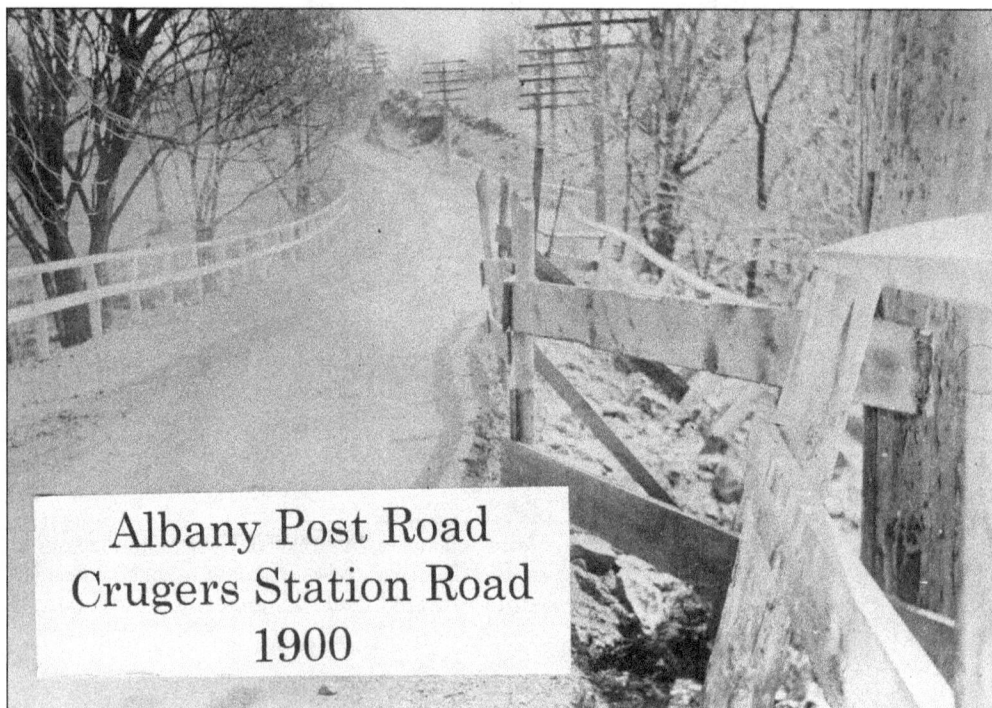

Albany Post Road
Crugers Station Road
1900

Seen here is the Albany Post Road at Crugers station as it appeared in 1900. (Courtesy of Henry Reynolds.)

This is a picture of barrels in the Ripley home, which stored apples, gourds, and other root vegetables. (Courtesy of Henry Reynolds.)

Here is a class of schoolchildren in the town of Cortlandt. There were often many ages within one class. The older children would assist the younger ones with their lessons. (Courtesy of Henry Reynolds.)

Here is an early home in Crugers, New York, with a driveway leading to the residence. (Courtesy of Henry Reynolds.)

Workers pause from creating the tunnel for the New York Central Railroad in Crugers, New York. The equipment used included a flatbed car and a crane. (Both, courtesy of Henry Reynolds.)

Tunnel workers and freight cars were part of the Hudson River railroad expansion. (Courtesy of Henry Reynolds.)

Early railroad construction shows a small sign marking the area known as Oscawana. (Both, courtesy of Henry Reynolds.)

Crugers Railroad Station, shown here in the 20th century, was a small train station on the early New York Central Railroad, now called Metro-North. The women pictured at the station appear in the long, flowing petticoats fashionable at the time. (Courtesy of Henry Reynolds.)

Early railroad expansion benefited both the upper and middle classes, providing jobs and the convenience of railroad travel. (Courtesy of Henry Reynolds.)

The New York Central Railroad was established in 1831. Above is a broad view of the railroad line. A conductor and some power lines are pictured below. (Both, courtesy of Henry Reynolds.)

The No. 34 Station is marked by railroad tracks and power lines. (Both, courtesy of Henry Reynolds.)

Early steam engines and freight cars were common along the Crugers railroad tracks. (Both, courtesy of Henry Reynolds.)

Mabel Palmer Ripley is shown here in her stylish, younger years on April 27, 1922. She maintained the Ripley homestead in Crugers. (Courtesy of Henry Reynolds.)

This man, sitting on a barrel, is surrounded by well-drilling apparatuses and a wagon. (Courtesy of Henry Reynolds.)

This well-drilling machinery and a pile of borings are evidence of Edwin Ripley's artesian well business around 1920. (Courtesy of Henry Reynolds.)

Artesian well drilling equipment includes pipes to allow underground water to rise to the top under pressure. (Courtesy of Henry Reynolds.)

The image above from 1919 shows a man with a "horseless carriage." The chickens are a reminder of Cortlandt's agricultural roots. The image below shows Crugers in 1922. (Both, courtesy of Henry Reynolds.)

In May 1919, Ripley's artesian well business was a unique addition to the community. (Both, courtesy of Henry Reynolds.)

Artesian wells, named for the French province of Artois, are centuries old in their technology. These photographs show Crugers in May 1919. (Courtesy of Henry Reynolds.)

For this successful enterprise, inspecting the boring pipes and machinery was necessary, as seen in this photograph taken on May 31, 1919. (Courtesy of Henry Reynolds.)

An up-close picture of the well demonstrates how this process of drilling is achieved. Note the huge wrench. (Courtesy of Henry Reynolds.)

A Model A or T car was certainly this man's pride and joy and a product of having a successful service of producing artesian wells in May 1922. (Courtesy of Henry Reynolds.)

On August 3, 1919, these three—most likely members of the Ripley family—enjoyed leisure time on their porch with pipe and newspaper, viewing the beautiful countryside with binoculars. (Both, courtesy of Henry Reynolds.)

Here, three people enjoy backyard time by looking through a telescope in Crugers in 1931. (Courtesy of Henry Reynolds.)

On April 22, 1923, three local men sat on a rock taking in the simple joy of a peaceful stream. (Both, courtesy of Henry Reynolds.)

Leisure time then was marked by quiet conversation among men who were more formally dressed than the activity would require, (Courtesy of Henry Reynolds.)

Here, two men in their strawhats hold a bore for an artesian well in July 1919. The water for these wells is naturally filtered because it passes through porous rock. (Courtesy of Henry Reynolds.)

In 1922, these men are standing in an open field, which was as treasured then as it is now in Crugers, New York. (Courtesy of Henry Reynolds.)

In November 1919, this bucolic riverfront image is marked by a stone wall and a bench for those wanting to enjoy this special place. (Courtesy of Henry Reynolds.)

This large house, with a pond and impressive pillars, was typical of estates found in Crugers. These residences were known for their comfortable living. (Both, courtesy of Henry Reynolds.)

Four

THE HAMLET
OF MONTROSE

Montrose, named for the Montross family, is a small hamlet located within the town of Cortlandt, specifically near Croton-on-Hudson and Verplanck in the northwestern corner of Westchester County.

As of the 2010 census, the population of Montrose was 3,487, but it has recently declined and is now estimated to be 2,701. The landform features include many wooded areas, ponds, and lakes. The Hudson River borders the hamlet on its western edge and is a source of both recreation and solace.

During the Abraham Lincoln administration, William Seward served as secretary of state and his son Frederick served as assistant secretary of state. While the elder Seward was recovering from a serious carriage accident, Frederick served as secretary of state.

Montrose is in the Hendrick Hudson School District (HHSD), formerly the Central School District No. 3. Within the hamlet of Montrose, there are the Hendrick Hudson High School and Frank G. Lindsey Elementary School. Other schools, which are in the HHSD but not in Montrose, include Blue Mountain Middle School, Buchanan-Verplanck Elementary School, and Furnace Woods Elementary School. The Hendrick Hudson Free Library is located at 185 Kings Ferry Road in Montrose and serves Buchanan, Verplanck, Crugers, and parts of Cortlandt Manor, Croton, and the city of Peekskill.

A local mecca of the town of Cortlandt and a historic feature is Cole's Market. The deli and butcher shop offers catering as well as the sale of individual sandwiches and salads. It sits in the center of the small built-up area of Montrose. Many local residents gather there to gossip and share the latest local news. A fire station, the site of an annual local parade, and a health club are also in Montrose. Montrose is home to the Franklin Delano Roosevelt campus of the Veterans' Affairs Healthcare System. Located on 50 sprawling acres, it was once the former site of the Dyckman home now known as Boscobel, a historic site in Garrison, New York.

Frederick W. Seward, son of William Seward, is shown with his family on the porch of their Montrose Point home. Both men would serve as secretary of state to Pres. Abraham Lincoln. (Courtesy of the Cortlandt Museum.)

Here is the Seward mansion at Montrose Point, New York. Note the distinct European architectural look and fine workmanship. The house no longer stands, and the property is most recently owned by the Catholic Kolping Society. (Courtesy of the Cortlandt Museum.)

In 1729, the Reformed Church of Cortlandtown was built on part of 172 acres. It burned down sometime between 1776 and 1785, possibly a victim of the American Revolution. (Courtesy of Barbara Annichairico.)

This undated postcard shows the men of Cortlandt Engine Company No. 1 of the Montrose Fire Department. The firehouse is centrally located on Albany Post Road in the hamlet. (Courtesy of Barbara Annichairico.)

This postcard shows the unpaved road to the Montrose depot. The depot no longer exists and has been replaced by the new Cortlandt train station. Visiting this station, one can see a group of three statues, which represent a Dutch patroon, a Mohican Indian, and a 19th-century brick carrier. They are iconic images of those who laid the groundwork for life in Cortlandt. (Courtesy of Barbara Annichairico.)

This is a photograph of the Montrose Elementary School in the winter of 1924. It would close its doors on March 18, 1957, and be replaced by Frank G. Lindsey Elementary School on trolley Road in Montrose. (Courtesy of Barbara Annichairico.)

This is the Episcopal Church of Divine Love on the corner of Sunset Road and Montrose Point Road. This Montrose house of worship has an adjoining cemetery and still serves the community to this day. (Courtesy of the Cortlandt Museum.)

Pastors and their families found a home not only in the parsonage at the Episcopal Church of Divine Love but also in this close-knit parish family. (Courtesy of the Cortlandt Museum.)

This photograph shows the Lent homestead on King's Ferry Road. There is also a Lent family cemetery in the town. Like many families in colonial times, the Lent family contained both Patriot and Tory members. (Courtesy of the Cortlandt Museum.)

This postcard shows the stately Lancaster residence in Montrose on the corner of King's Ferry Road and Lent Avenue. The postmark on this card is October 29, 1908. (Courtesy of the Cortlandt Museum.)

Almost unrecognizable by today's standards, this is Route 9A as a dirt road with a grocery store on the right, north of Dutch Street. Dutch Street honors the many families who came from Holland, such as the Verplancks and the VanCortlandts, and settled in the town. (Courtesy of the Cortlandt Museum.)

The Reynolds residence sustained significant damage after a cyclone hit in 1907. It is interesting to note the use of the word "cyclone" on the photograph as opposed to a hurricane. (Courtesy of the Cortlandt Museum.)

Damage from the cyclone on Dutch Street in Montrose in 1907 shows a unique occurrence—houses on one side of the street were left untouched while those nearby were destroyed. (Courtesy of the Cortlandt Museum.)

Pictured here is the Grace Charles house at King's Ferry Road and Lent Avenue. The home is representative of those fine pieces of architecture that can be so rare. (Courtesy of the Cortlandt Museum.)

Frank Mason's Montrose Dairy Products were purveyors of wholesale butter, eggs, and cheese. Note the phone number using words instead of numbers for the phone exchange. Delivering country goods to city residents was a treat as well as a necessity. (Courtesy of the Cortlandt Museum.)

One of these houses was the Lent homestead located on King's Ferry Road between Lent and Harper Avenues. Evelyn Lent notes on the postcard that the house on the right is the family home. (Courtesy of the Cortlandt Museum.)

In 1931–1932, the Hendrick Hudson High School girls' basketball team posed for this photograph. An unidentified gentleman is pictured with the players. Members of the team are, from left to right, (first row) Catherine Tice, Edwina Gibson, Catherine Chopyak, Catherine ?, ? Vulgum, Esther Balogh, and Evelyn Ingold; (second row) Vera Botens, Ethel Monroe, Barbara Jamison, Anna Matlock, Mary Jones, Emily J. Tuttle, Marion Terbush, and Agnes Behrens. Emily (née Tuttle) Lent would go on to be a reading teacher at Frank G. Lindsey School for more than 50 years. (Courtesy of the Field Library Local History Collection, the Colin T. Naylor Jr. Archives.)

Printed in the *Evening Star* newspaper, local historian Colin Naylor stated, "Augustus J. Cole, President of The Board of Education of Central School District No. 3, broke ground for the new Hendrick Hudson High School in 1926." This locale was developing rapidly, with construction of this school beginning the next chapter in public schooling. Naylor identified the people as follows: "From left to right are Mr. Kell, the contractor, Frank G. Lindsey, Supervising Principal, Thomas Nolan, Board President Cole, David Henion, James H. Chase, James H. Ferris and George Welch, longtime district clerk." Treasurer Howard Conklin was unable to attend the ground-breaking. Frank G. Lindsey would later have a local school named in his honor. The newspaper article by Naylor is held in the William J. Burke History Collection at Buchanan Village Hall. (Courtesy of Tina Rickett.)

BASE BALL SCHEDULE
For Season of 1925

Roosevelt
High School

BUCHANAN
NEW YORK

CARMEN MORETTI..........*Captain*
FRANK HANIFY..........*Manager*

Roosevelt High School, now Hendrick Hudson High School, published this baseball schedule in 1925. Much like today, participation in sports was part of a well-rounded education. Team pride instilled morals as well as a good sense of cooperation, which helped students move into adulthood. (Courtesy of the Cortlandt Museum.)

Roosevelt High School Base Ball Schedule for Season of 1925

	R.	Op.		R.	p.
Wednesday, April 8 MOHEGAN ....Away	12	8	*Friday, May 15* WASHINGTON IRVING At Home	8	7
Wednesday, April 15 YONKERS ....At Home	9	7	*Tuesday, May 19* PEEKSKILL H.S......Away	8	9
may *Thursday, April 16* PEEKSKILL M.A......Away	8	9	*Wednesday, May 20* OAKWOOD ....Away	9	10
Friday, April 24 OSSINING ....Away	6	9	*Friday, May 22* No. TARRYTOWN..At Home	8	6
Tuesday, April 28 WASHINGTON IRVING.Away	10	14	*Saturday, May 30* OAKWOOD ....At Home		
Tuesday, May 5 PEEKSKILL H.S...At Home	8	7	*June 3* *George Washington - Away* *Saturday, June 6* EVANDER CHILDS . At Home		
Friday, May 8 No. TARRYTOWN.....Away	1	10			
Tuesday, May 12 OSSINING ....At Home	11	5	*Saturday, June 13* GEORGE WASHINGTON At Home		

94

This original photograph is of a Montrose Elementary School class. Mr. Gilmore was the teacher of these students in the school located on Dutch Street around 1887. Bertha Hunt (left) and Minnie Taniggar are standing in front of the teacher at the top center of this image. The school was part of District No. 15, which would later become Central School District No. 3. (Courtesy of Barbara Annichairico.)

Ornate desks are pictured in this classroom at Montrose Elementary School in the autumn of 1913. The serious expressions on the students' faces were common at the time. (Courtesy of Barbara Annichairico.)

In April 1920, students of the Montrose Elementary School pose for this photograph. Two names are noted on the original image: Stanton and Phil Cole. Note the large class size and various dresses at the time. Girls often wore dresses to school and large bows in their hair. (Courtesy of Barbara Annichairico.)

Barbara Annichairico notes the following in this school photograph from Montrose, New York: Ethelda Croft, Barbara's aunt Elva, Chase Turnis, Claus and John Aldoubt. Mr. Rabe (the principal), a Woodworth, a Winn girl, and Mary Reynolds Brigham. (Courtesy of Barbara Annichairico.)

Dressed in their finest and ready to take their places in the world, members of the Hendrick Hudson High School class of 1938 pose for a photograph. The high school, built in 1926, still stands today in Montrose on Albany Post Road. (Courtesy of Diane Edwards Tangen.)

Children in Miss Harlow's class at Montrose Elementary School sit with perfect posture and hands clasped in 1913. (Courtesy of Barbara Annichairico.)

This is a photograph of a school trip during the 1950–1951 school year. Hendrick Hudson High School student Diane (née Edwards) Tangen is at the far right in the first row. (Courtesy of Diane Edwards Tangen.)

The Senior Class
of
Hendrick Hudson High School
announces
Class Night-Friday, June twenty-first
Commencement-Monday, June twenty-fourth
at eight fifteen o'clock
High School Auditorium
Montrose, New York

Tommy

HENDRICK HUDSON HIGH SCHOOL

Pictured here is an invitation to a Hendrick Hudson High School commencement for the class of 1957. The program of events for that weekend is listed in the invitation. (Courtesy of Tommy Cole Jr.)

Tom Cole Sr. and Geraldine Teed pose happily for their wedding photograph. They were high school sweethearts from Hendrick Hudson High School and became parents of four wonderful children: Christine, Tommy Jr., Trish, and Robby. (Courtesy of Tommy Cole Jr.)

Parent's Signature

1st Report	_Mrs. Lester Teed_
2nd Report	_Mrs. Lester Teed_
3rd Report	_Mrs. Lester Teed_
4th Report	_Mrs. Lester Teed_
Promoted to	_4th Grade_
Teacher	_Helene Dixon_

Central School District, No. 3

FRANK G. LINDSEY, Supervising Principal

PUPIL PROGRESS CARD
for the Primary Grades

September 1945 to June 1946

Pupil's Name _Teed, Geraldine_

Grade _Three_

School _Mc Kinley_

1st Report—Ending October 31
2nd Report—Ending December 31
3rd Report—Ending February 28
4th Report—Ending April 30
5th Report—Ending June ....

Principal _Helen Gedney_

Teacher _Helene Dixon_

Geraldine Teed was a student at Mckinley School in the Hendrick Hudson School District for the 1945–1946 school year, and she did well. This report card reflects the school's interest in the whole child along with test results. (Courtesy of Tommy and Trish Cole.)

Progress in School Subjects

E—Excellent S—Satisfactory P—Poor (Promotion Doubtful) F—Failing

	1	2	3	4	5
Expression — Oral	S	S	S	S	S
Handwork	S	S	S	S	S
Music	S	S	S	S	S
Number Work	E	E	E	E	E
Reading — Oral	S	S	E	E	E
Reading — Word Recognition	S	S	E	F	E
Reading — Comprehension	S	E	E	E	E
Spelling (No marks in Gr. 1)	E	E	E	E	E
Writing	S	S	S	S	S

Remarks

1. Geraldine is doing nice work.
2. Her work is well done.
3. She is doing very well.
4. Work is nicely done.

Character Building Habits

	1	2	3	4	5
Co-operation	E	E	E	E	E
Dependability (a) Consideration for school property	E	E	E	E	E
(b) In doing assigned tasks	E	E	E	E	E
Effort	E	E	E	E	E

Rate of Progress

	1	2	3	4	5
Rapid					
Normal	✓	✓	✓	✓	✓
Slow					

Attendance

	1	2	3	4	5
Days Absent	0	0	0	0	2

Health

	1	2	3	4	5
Daily Health Inspection	P	P	P	P	S

Defects Found by School Doctor

None.

Remarks on Health

Bites her nails.

The University of the State of New York

𝔓𝔯𝔢𝔩𝔦𝔪𝔦𝔫𝔞𝔯𝔶 ℭ𝔢𝔯𝔱𝔦𝔣𝔦𝔠𝔞𝔱𝔢

Be it known that

June 14-18   19 *26*

David Cole

Satisfactorily completed the requirements for admission to academic grade by passing examinations in the following subjects at

Buchanan Union School

| READING | WRITING | SPELLING | ELEMENTARY ENGLISH | ARITHMETIC |
| GEOGRAPHY | | | ELEMENTARY U. S. HISTORY | |

Geo. M. Wiley,

Assistant Commissioner for Elementary Education

No. *3424* on the school records

Frank G. Lindsey Principal

This certificate of achievement for David Cole Jr., a brother of Tom Cole Sr., was awarded in June 1926. The principal at the time of this "Buchanan Union School" was Frank G. Lindsey. Later, he was honored in Montrose with a school named for him, the Frank G. Lindsey Elementary School. (Courtesy of Tommy Cole Jr.)

This second-grade class at Frank G. Lindsey School in 1971 counts Tommy Cole Jr., third row, second from the left, as one of its students. Second from the left is teacher Carol Frank. (Courtesy of Tommy Cole Jr.)

Pictured here in 1973 is Tommy Cole Jr.'s fourth-grade class as well as teacher Sue Donnell. (Courtesy of Tommy Cole Jr.)

In the early 20th century, this photograph shows Montrose residents celebrating and having a night out. Mary Edith Cole, grandmother of Tommy Cole Jr., is sitting at the far right; everyone else is unidentified. (Courtesy of Tommy Cole Jr.)

Pictured here are several Montrose residents in formal dress at an apparent party in the early 20th century. (Courtesy of Tommy Cole Jr.)

Pictured are, from left to right, brothers David Cole Jr. and Tom Cole Sr. and Carol Ann Tice. The Cole family would later create a local business that thrives to this day. (Courtesy of Trish and Tommy Cole Jr.)

Tommy Cole Jr.'s father, Tom Cole Sr., is pictured here at the age of two years and nine months. (Courtesy of Tommy Cole Jr.)

Tom Cole Sr., age one year and eleven months, plays in his backyard in Montrose, New York. (Courtesy of the Cole family.)

Tom Cole Sr. is pictured here in 1966 with Tommy Jr. and his sister Christine. (Courtesy of the Cole family.)

In July 1911, this young boy's outfit was the norm. This hat has been passed down through the Cole family. (Courtesy of the Cole family.)

This is an image of young fishermen, ages six and four, from the Cole family photograph collection. (Courtesy of the Cole family.)

This is believed to be George Keefe at the age of two. (Courtesy of the Cole family.)

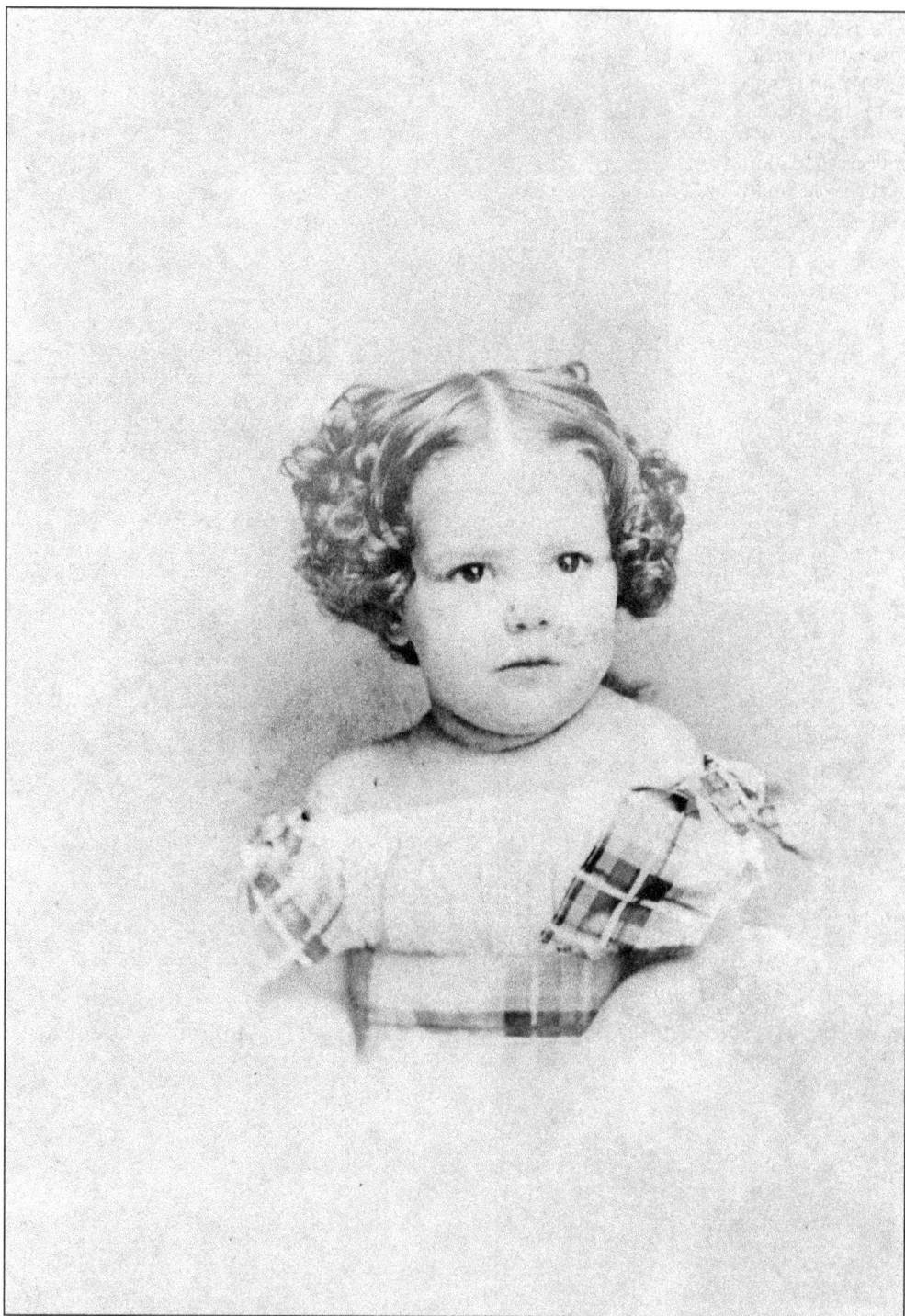

This is a *carte de visite*, which was popular from the mid-19th century and was used to advertise the photographic talents of a local studio in capturing a special person or occasion. This is little Florence in 1864. Rockwood photographers in New York City produced this card. (Courtesy of Judy O'Brien.)

This early-20th-century woman wears the stern expression and high-collared dress fashionable at the time. She is an unidentified resident of Montrose, New York. (Courtesy of Tom Cole Jr.)

This early photograph of an unidentified Montrose man was found among the Cole family photographs. (Courtesy of the Cole family.)

Eric Peterson and his orchestra were part of the big band era, which was a universal craze. (Courtesy of the Cole family.)

ERIC PETERSON
AND HIS
ORCHESTRA

The Eric Peterson Orchestra was also known as "the stylist of modern dance music." David Cole Jr. (standing on the right below the staircase), the brother of Tom Cole Sr., played a brass instrument in the internationally famous orchestra. (Courtesy of the Cole family.)

This is a Montrose boy, most likely his school photograph, in the mid-20th century. (Courtesy of the Cole family.)

This is an early photograph of Cole's Market on Albany Post Road in Montrose. (Courtesy of the Cole family.)

Here is an early-20th-century home in Montrose. The following is found on the back of the photograph: "Remember the old Jersey sweet apple tree and the big cedar tree around 1902–1905 gas station there now, house was moved back." (Courtesy of Barbara Annichairico.)

Young at heart, two adults enjoy a childhood pastime—snow ball fighting! (Courtesy of Henry Reynolds.)

Five

THE HAMLET OF VERPLANCK

Verplanck, named for Phillip Verplanck, who was married to a VanCortlandt, is one of the oldest, most-storied areas in the town of Cortlandt. As early as 1664, a major river crossing ran from "the point," across the Hudson River, to the north side of Stony Point. People traveling through the original colonies used this as a ferry crossing. In fact, the road that connects Montrose to Verplanck is called King's Ferry Road.

Phillip Verplanck built a house on a bluff overlooking the Hudson River where he and his family of nine children resided until the house was shelled and burned by a British warship during the American Revolution.

The close river access of Verplanck led to its early economic development and contributed to its prosperity. When clay deposits were found in Verplanck, brick making and brickyards flourished. By the end of the 19th century, the deposits of sand and clay were being depleted, forcing the closing of many brickyards.

Another major contributor in the development of Verplanck again centers on the Hudson River. The docks were used for steamboats traveling the river between New York City and Albany. Steamboat Dock is a well-known gathering place on the Hudson River shore in Verplanck. Later, there were seaplanes landing and traveling in this area of town. Additionally, a stagecoach route connected Verplanck to neighboring Peekskill, three miles north. The stage was replaced by a trolley, and Trolley Road in the hamlet of Montrose, where the trolley traveled, bears its name.

For more than 100 years, fishing was a major and important activity in Verplanck. Its extensive shoreline and location always encouraged river activity. Sturgeon, crabs, and shad roe were caught and sold commercially in New York City's Fulton Fish Market.

Educationally, one of the earliest schools in Westchester County was built in Verplanck in 1876 for the "modest" amount of $8,000. While no longer a school, the building still stands and is used for community activities. Students now attend Buchanan-Verplanck Elementary School on Westchester Avenue.

Verplanck has stories to tell, is steeped in history and tradition, and is surrounded by natural riverside beauty.

The Croton Historical Society donated this photograph of brick makers in Verplanck in 1897 to the Bear Mountain Toll House Visitor Information Center. Note the three shoeless young boys on the right; child labor was an unfortunate part of the workforce at this time. (Courtesy of Laura Lee M. Keating.)

Here is Empire Grove in Verplanck in the 1950s. Empire Grove, aptly named after New York State's nickname—the Empire State, was a parkland area in Verplanck. It housed and sponsored recreational facilities for the community. (Courtesy of Cheryl and William Murray.)

116

EMPIRE GROVE, VERPLANCKS, N. Y.

Steamboats also provided convenient transportation to Empire Grove for a day of outdoor fun and relaxation. (Courtesy of Cheryl and William Murray.)

VERPLANCK'S POINT ON THE HUDSON
(STONY POINT PARK IN THE FOREGROUND)

SITE FOR THE
PERMANENT INTERNATIONAL EXPOSITION
1609—HUDSON-FULTON CELEBRATION—1909

Here is another commemorative image of Verplanck's Point in Verplanck. (Courtesy of Cheryl and William Murray.)

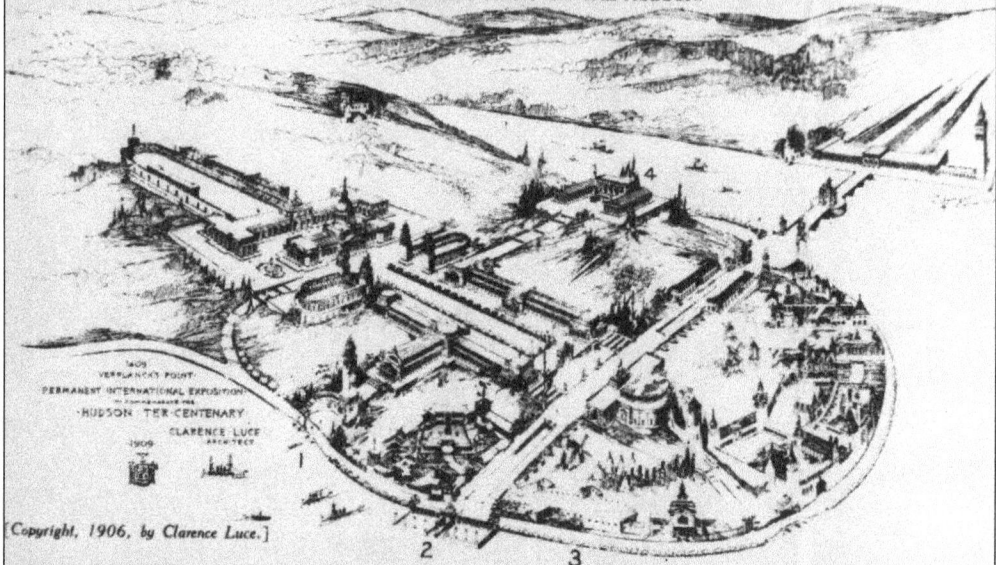

COME TO THE OPENING OF NEW YORK'S EXPOSITION IN 190?
AT VERPLANCK'S POINT ON THE HUDSON.

1909
VERPLANCK POINT
PERMANENT INTERNATIONAL EXPOSITION
·HUDSON· TER-CENTENARY·
CLARENCE LUCE
ARCHITECT
1909

[Copyright, 1906, by Clarence Luce.]

s point Henry Hudson first cast anchor in October, 1609, and from this point, in 1807, the inhabitants of Verplanck witnessed
ver of Fulton's steamboat, the "Claremont."
ing's Ferry Landing, over which more troops passed, during the Revolutionary War, than at any other spot in the country.
are the ruins of the water battery erected by the Americans to resist the British fleet.
is hill George Washington reviewed the French troops under Count Rochambeau, upon their return, in 1781, from the victory

This is a map showing the plans for a grand Hudson-Fulton Exposition in 1909. It would become a permanent park on Verplanck's Hudson River shoreline. (Courtesy of Cheryl and William Murray.)

These trolley conductors on the tracks in Verplanck gave residents the opportunity to travel "uptown" to Peekskill to shop in its quaint stores. (Courtesy of Judy O'Brien.)

118

Here is a closer look at the 1910 trolley, which traveled from Verplanck. The Frank G. Lindsey School is located on Trolley Road in Montrose. (Courtesy of Cheryl and William Murray.)

Pictured is White Beach on the shores of the Hudson River in Verplanck. (Courtesy of Cheryl and William Murray.)

This postcard image shows a local marching band in a Verplanck parade. (Courtesy of Judy O'Brien.)

Members of the ladies' auxiliary from St. Patrick's Church march proudly in their crisp white uniforms. (Courtesy of Judy O'Brien.)

St. Patrick's Church, Verplancks, Westchester Co., New York, 1880.

St. Patrick's Church was a cornerstone in Verplanck in 1880. Note the icehouse in the front. (Courtesy of Cheryl and William Murray.)

Trolley tracks in Verplanck are no obstacle for this man walking his cow. (Courtesy of Judy O'Brien.)

Closing Exercises

—OF—

The Verplancks Public School,

FRIDAY, JUNE 27, 1884,

At 1:30 P. M.

COMMITTEE.

Annie C. Curtis,	Agnes T. Hard,	Theressa Kelly,
James J. Vaughey,	Maggie T. Donohue,	Mary Farrey,
	Agnes McGuire.	

BOARD OF EDUCATION.

Christopher Vaughey,
Michael Curtis,
Philip O'Brien,

Henry S Purdy, Principal,
Alice P. Burnes,
Mary E. Shanahan,
Mary E. McGuire.

This is a program of the closing exercises of the Verplancks Public School on Friday, June 24, 1884. This original program features many names that are still found in the area today. (Both, courtesy of Judy O'Brien.)

PROGRAMME.

1 Salutatory, - Agnes McGuire
2 A Happy Greeting to All, - School
3 The Holiday, - Joseph Waugh
4 The Blind Brother, - Geo. Rothwiler
5 Little by Little, - Matthew McGuire
6 The Colliers Dying Child, - Kate McPartlan
7 Mill May—Song, - Primary Department
8 The Captains Daughter, - Mary Rogan
9 Water, - Emma Waugh
10 Creeping up the Stairs, - Sadie Martin
11 Carry this kiss to Mother, - Mary Murphy
12 Johnny lost, - Harry Hard
13 He never told a Lie—Song, -
14 The Light on the Shore, - Lewis H. Bleakley
15 Granpa's Darling, - Mary Balan
16 Weighing the Baby, - Mary J. Heeney
17 Shadows, - Teressa Kelly
18 The Dying Child, - Lizzie Martin
19 Twins, - Katie Meaney
20 Clap, Clap, Hurrah, - Primary Department
21 Land of Washington, - Willie King
22 Only a Little Brook, - Tillie Long
23 Trip Lightly, - Christie Vaughey
24 Good Night, - Laura Tuttle
25 I Love you so, - Bridget Brown
26 The Unfinished Prayer, - Ellen Brown
27 Students Lay—Song, - Intermediate
28 The Stab, - James V. Kelly
29 Not Married yet, - Gustave Henry

30 The Sword of Bunker-hill, - James J. Vaughey
31 The Child's first Grief, - Sarah Murray
32 Too late for School, - Mary McGill
33 The Rainy Day, - Chorus
34 Having and Giving, - Susie Timoney
35 The Lost Nestlings, - Rose A. McGill
36 Song of the Shirt, - Agnes T. Hard
37 The Dead Child's, Ford, - Clara Timoney
38 Nobody's Child, - Gussie Williamson
39 There's none like a Mother, - Mary McGee
40 Sheridan's Ride, - Mary Farrey
41 Battle Hymn of the Republic, - Chorus
42 Somebody's Mother, - ...ie Farrey
43 The Sale, - Annie C. Curtis
44 Spring Clothing, - Agnes McGuire / Gustave Henry
45 The Dying Californian, - Julia Boyle
46 Solitude, - Annie Kelly
47 Nothing to do, - Maggie Donohue
48 The Pic-Nic, - Hannah Driscoll
49 The Drunkard's Dream, - Lizzie Martin
50 Contentment, - Mamie Martin
51 A Smack in School, - Mary Farrey
52 Barbara Frietchie, - Jas. J. Vaughey
53 Star Spangled Banner, - Chorus
54 A Kiss at the Door, - Teressa Kelly
55 Bingen on the Rhine, - Annie C. Curtis
56 Be quiet—I'll tell my Mother, - Agnes Hard
57 Wishing, - Chorus.

Here, skaters enjoy the frozen Lake Meahagh in Verplanck in January 1941. (Courtesy of the Cortlandt Museum.)

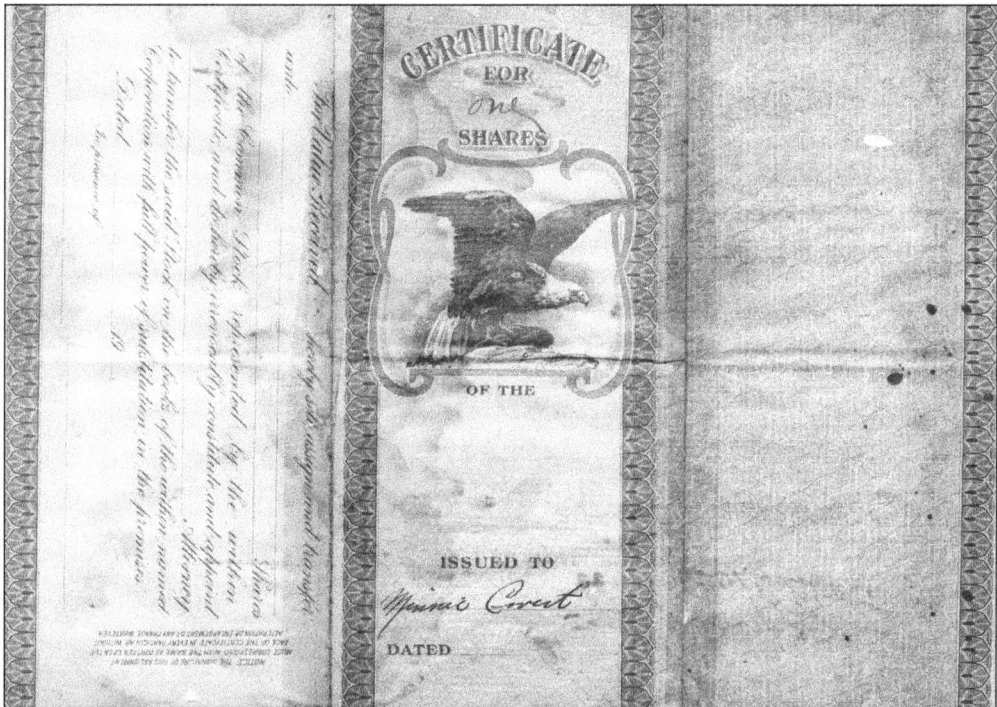

The Verplanck and Tompkins Cove Ferry Company, Inc., presented these impressive stock certificates to shareholders in September 1923. (Courtesy of the Cortlandt Museum.)

Visit us at
arcadiapublishing.com

www.ingramcontent.com/pod-product-compliance
Lightning Source LLC
Chambersburg PA
CBHW080616110426

42813CB00006B/1520

* 9 7 8 1 5 3 1 6 7 1 9 3 8 *